I Know Someone with Autism

Sue Barraclough

Heinemann Library
Chicago, Illinois

www.heinemannraintree.com
Visit our website to find out more information about Heinemann-Raintree books.

To order:

☎ Phone 888-454-2279

🖥 Visit www.heinemannraintree.com to browse our catalog and order online.

Edited by Rebecca Rissman, Daniel Nunn, and Siân Smith
Designed by Joanna Hinton Malivoire
Picture research by Mica Brancic
Originated by Capstone Global Library
Printed and bound in China by South China Printing Co.Ltd

15 14 13 12 11
10 9 8 7 6 5 4 3 2 1

Library of Congress Cataloging-in-Publication Data
Barraclough, Sue.
  I know someone with autism / Sue Barraclough.
    p. cm. — (Understanding health issues)
  Includes bibliographical references and index.
  ISBN 978-1-4329-4563-3 (hc)
  ISBN 978-1-4329-4579-4 (pb)
  1. Autism—Juvenile literature. I. Title.
  RC553.A88B369 2011
  616.85'882—dc22   2010026579

Acknowledgments
We would like to thank the following for permission to reproduce photographs: Alamy p. 22 (© Lyndsay Russell); Corbis p. 16 (© Grady Reese); Getty Images pp. 12 (PhotoAlto/Eric Audras), 13 (Dorling Kindersley/Andy Crawford), 14 (Photographer's Choice/Mieke Dalle), 23 (Fuse), 25 (Tetra Images), 26 (WireImage/John Shearer); iStockphoto pp. 4 left (© Eileen Hart), 14 (© Chris Schmidt); Photolibrary pp. 5 (BSIP Medical/Laurent/Helen), 6 (Brand X Pictures), 8 (Juice Images), 15 (Paul Doyle), 19 (Flirt Collection/Michael Prince), 20 (Alexis Maryon), 21 (imagebroker.net/Michael Peuckert), 24 (Tetra Images/Jetta Productions/Walter Hodges); Rex Features p. 27 (Everett Collection); Shutterstock pp. 4 right (© Adrian Hughes), 11 (© John McLaird), 17 (© Igor Kisselev), 18 (© Yevgen Kotyukh).

Cover photograph of a boy working on a pottery wheel reproduced with permission of Getty Images (The Image Bank/John Kelly).

We would like to thank Matthew Siegel and Ashley Wolinski for their invaluable help in the preparation of this book.

Contents

Some words are printed in bold, **like this**. You can find out what they mean in the glossary.

Do You Know Someone with Autism?

Do you have any friends who have autism? Some people with autism cannot **communicate** well. They may find it hard to understand other people and what they mean.

Some people with autism may not realize that a smile can mean someone feels happy, or a frown can mean that someone feels sad.

Being in a new place can be
difficult for a person with autism.

Some people with autism can be upset
by changes. Many people do not like
change, but this does not mean they are
autistic. Someone with autism may find
change very worrying or even scary.

What Is Autism?

Autism is a **condition** that affects how people see and act with the world. There are many different types and levels of autism. This is known as the **autistic spectrum**.

Some people with autism like to always do daily tasks, such as doing the dishes or going to bed, exactly the same way.

Every person with autism is different. Some people with autism never learn to talk. Some people have such mild autism that they never even know that they have it.

Having autism can mean:
- hating change and liking **routines**
- not liking to meet new people or do new activities
- avoiding **eye contact**
- saying the same thing or doing the same thing over and over
- focusing on one object or one activity.

What Causes Autism?

Nobody is really sure what causes autism. Autism may be **genetic**. This means it is passed from parents to their children. It is not possible to catch autism from another person.

Autism is part of who a person is.

Certain parts of the brain control different activities, such as moving, feeling, thinking, and talking. Scientists think that parts of the brain develop differently in a person who has autism.

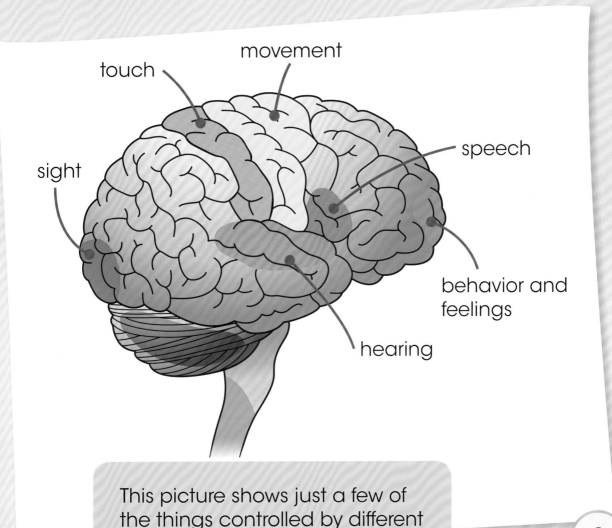

touch

movement

sight

speech

behavior and feelings

hearing

This picture shows just a few of the things controlled by different parts of our brains.

Understanding Autism

Someone with autism may not understand that somebody else feels happy or upset.

Some people with autism find it hard to understand how other people feel. For example, they might laugh if someone is hurt. They are not being mean. They just do not understand how other people feel.

Many people with autism move differently. People with autism may rock, flap their hands, jump up and down, or make faces. Movements like this make a person with autism feel safe and in control.

Repeating movements sometimes helps people with autism to let out their feelings.

Feelings About Change

Some people with autism like to do things in a certain way. They might get angry or upset if a **routine** is changed. A routine makes them feel safe and in control.

Some people with autism find it important to do things in a certain way or in the same order.

People with autism may like things to stay the same. They might get upset if things are moved.

Some people with autism find changes or having to do new things very worrying. It can help if they know about changes that are going to happen. It is important for others to understand that change can be difficult for someone with autism.

Communication

People need to pass information on to each other all the time. This is called **communication**. Many people with autism need help to communicate better. They may need to learn simple skills such as making **eye contact**.

If you look at people while they are talking, it helps to show them that you are listening.

We can learn lots of different ways to communicate.

Having support at an early age can help many children with autism learn to talk. Some people with autism are not able to talk, but they can learn **sign language** or use pictures to communicate.

Some people have a form of autism called **Asperger's**. Many people with Asperger's can learn and **communicate** well, but they have problems with **social skills**. These skills are related to how we understand others and make friends.

People with Asperger's can have difficulty understanding what people mean or how they feel.

Someone with autism may be more sensitive to loud noises.

Many people with autism need special help because they experience the world differently. For someone with autism, sights, smells, or sounds can be very strong.

Strengths and Support

Many people with autism can have special strengths and talents. For example, they may be able to play a piece of music after only hearing it once, or be able to remember long lists of information.

Some people with autism are very talented artists.

Everyone has different strengths and weaknesses. People with autism also have different things they do well. They may also need different kinds of help.

Different people enjoy doing different things.

Living with Autism

Special teachers can give support and teach different skills.

There is no **cure** for autism, but people can learn ways to overcome some of the difficulties they have. People with autism can learn new skills that will help them in the future. They can find ways of controlling difficult behaviors.

It is important that children with autism get help and support as early as possible. People with autism can often learn to be independent and go on to have jobs and families of their own.

This woman worked hard to become a vet.

Being a Good Friend

Autism affects people differently. Some people with autism hate to be touched, while others love to be hugged tightly. Some people with autism hate bright colors, while others love them. Some people with autism enjoy loud noises, while others find them scary.

Good friends understand each other.

You can help by understanding that a friend with autism may not want to join in games and other group activities.

You can be a good friend by learning about the things your friend likes and how he or she wants to be treated. A person with autism often likes places that are quiet and familiar. You can help by making sure your friend feels safe.

How Can I Help?

People with autism may not always understand some words or phrases. For example, if you said that you "laughed your head off" they might find it scary. You can help a friend with autism by speaking plainly and simply.

If a friend finds something difficult to understand, try to explain it in a different way.

You can help friends with autism to learn and discover things they can do well.

Some people with autism are very good at subjects such as math, art, and music. They can also be very good at concentrating on one activity. This often means they can learn to do it very well.

Famous People with Autism

Jason McElwain found out he had autism when he was young, and he struggled to make friends at school. He worked hard to improve his **social skills** and got involved with the school basketball team. Jason now helps to raise money for autism research.

Jason McElwain became famous when he played for 4 minutes at the end of a basketball game and scored 20 points.

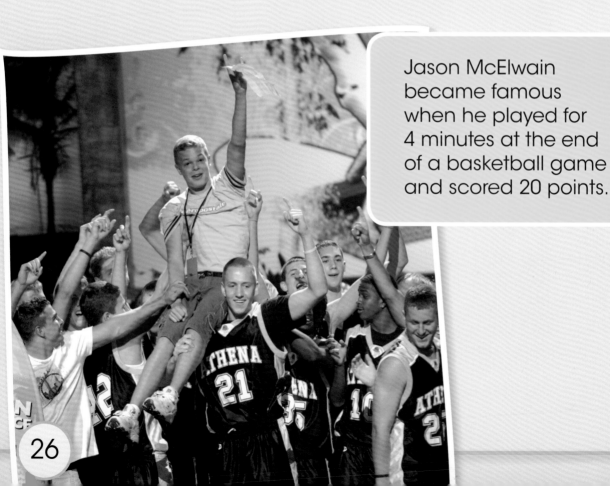

One of the most famous of Daryl Hannah's movies is about a mermaid who is found washed up on a beach.

Daryl Hannah's parents were told she was borderline autistic when she was very young. She later became an actress and has starred in many successful movies.

Autism: True or False?

People with autism are unfriendly. They do not want to make friends.

FALSE! People with autism want to have friends, but they sometimes find it difficult to talk to strangers and are not sure how to act.

There are four times as many boys as girls with autism.

TRUE! More boys than girls have autism.

You cannot catch autism from another person.

TRUE! It is not possible to catch autism from someone else.

It is the parents' fault that children have autism. A child with autism is just behaving badly.

FALSE! Autism has nothing to do with the way a child is brought up. A child with autism cannot help behaving differently.

Glossary

Asperger's type of autism in which a person has difficulties with social skills and finds it hard to understand how people feel

autistic spectrum name for the wide range of different types and levels of autism

communicate pass information on

condition something that affects the way some parts of the body work

cure medical treatment that makes someone better

eye contact looking into someone's eyes

genetic something that is passed on from parents to their children

routine set order for doing things

sign language way of communicating using hands and fingers

social skills skills used for understanding people and making friends

Find Out More

Books to Read

Adams, Sue. *A Book About What Autism Can Be Like*. Philadelphia: Jessica Kingsley, 2009.

Doering Tourville, Amanda. *My Friend Has Austism (Friends with Disabilities)*. Mankato, Minn.: Picture Window, 2010.

Shapiro, Ouisie. *Autism and Me: Sibling Stories*. Morton Grove, Ill.: Albert Whitman, 2009.

Websites

http://kidshealth.org/kid/health_problems/brain/autism.html
Visit Kids' Health to learn more about autism.

www.autism-society.org
The Autistic Society of America website has lots of information about autism and Asperger's, along with links to other useful organizations.

Index